Gardening in the Tropics

BOOKS BY OLIVE SENIOR

POETRY
Talking of Trees
Gardening in the Tropics
Over the Roofs of the World

SHORT STORIES
Summer Lightning
Arrival of the Snake-Woman
Discerner of Hearts

NON-FICTION
A-Z of Jamaican Heritage
*Working Miracles: Women's Lives in the English-Speaking
Caribbean*
Encyclopedia of Jamaican Heritage

Gardening in the Tropics
Olive Senior

A 4 A.M. BOOK

INSOMNIAC PRESS

Library and Archives Canada Cataloguing in Publication
Senior, Olive
Gardening in the tropics / Olive Senior.

Poems.
Originally published: Toronto: McClelland and Stewart, 1994.
ISBN 1-897178-00-X

I. Title.
PS8587.E552G37 2005   C811'.54   C2005-903423-8

First published in Canada by McClelland & Stewart (1994)
and in Great Britain by Bloodaxe Books (1995).

The publisher gratefully acknowledges the support of the
Canada Council, the Ontario Arts Council and the
Department of Canadian Heritage through the Book
Publishing Industry Development Program.

Printed and bound in Canada
Insomniac Press
192 Spadina Avenue, Suite 403
Toronto, Ontario, Canada, M5T 2C2
www.insomniacpress.com

CONTENTS

Gourd   7

TRAVELLERS' TALES
Meditation on Yellow   11
Hurricane Story, 1903   19
Moonshine Dolly   22
Hurricane Story, 1944   24
Cat's Cradle   28
Caribbean Basin Initiative   29
Hurricane Story, 1951   35
Illegal Immigrant   44
Stowaway   45
Meditation on Red   46
Hurricane Story, 1988   56
All Clear, 1928   57

NATURE STUDIES
Plants   63
Starapple   65
Pineapple   66
Madam Fate   68
Fern   69
Mountain Pride   70
Sun and Moon   71
Snail   72
Guava   73
Guava/2   74
Guinep   75
Anatto and Guinep   76
Pawpaw   78
Bamboo (*In Five Variations*)   79

GARDENING IN THE TROPICS

Brief Lives   85
My Father's Blue Plantation   86
Finding Your Stone   87
The Knot Garden   88
The Colours of Birds   90
The Tree of Life   93
Seeing the Light   95
Amazon Women   97
Tropic Love   100
The Immovable Tenant   101
Gardening on the Run   107
Advice and Devices   111

MYSTERY

Marassa: Divine Twins   117
Obatala: Father of Wisdom   118
Osanyin: God of Herbalism   119
Ososi: God of Hunting   120
Ogun: God of Iron   121
Shango: God of Thunder   123
Orunmilla: God of Divination   126
Babalu: Lord of the Earth   127
Oya: Goddess of the Wind   129
Olokun: God of the Deep Ocean   130
Yemoja: Mother of Waters   133
Guédé: Lord of the Dead   136

Acknowledgements   139

g
o
gourd
r
d
hollowed dried
calabash humble took-took
how simple you look. But what
lies beneath that crusty exterior?
Such stories they tell! They say O packy,
in your youth (before history), as cosmic
container, you ordered divination, ritual
sounds, incantations, you were tomb, you were
womb, you were heavenly home, the birthplace of
life here on earth. Yet broken (they say) you
caused the first Flood. Indiscretion could release
from inside you again the scorpion of darkness that
once covered the world. The cosmic snake (it is said)
strains to hold you together for what chaos would ensue
if heaven and earth parted! They say there are those
who've been taught certain secrets: how to harness the
power of your magical enclosure by the ordering of sound
– a gift from orehu the spirit of water who brought the
first calabash and the stones for the ritual, who taught
how to fashion the heavenly rattle, the sacred Mbaraká,
that can summon the spirits and resound cross the abyss
– like the houngan's asson or the shaman's maraka. Yet
hollowed dried calabash, humble took-took, we've walked
far from that water, from those mystical shores. If
all we can manage is to rattle our stones, our
beads or our bones in your dried-out container,
in shak-shak or maracca, will our voices
be heard? If we dance to your rhythm,
knock-knock on your skin, will we
hear from within, no matter
how faintly, your
wholeness
resound?

hollowed
dried
calabash
humble
took-took

how simple

you look

TRAVELLERS' TALES

MEDITATION ON YELLOW

"The yellow of the Caribbean seen from Jamaica at
three in the afternoon."
– Gabriel García Márquez

I

At three in the afternoon
you landed here at El Dorado
(for heat engenders gold and
fires the brain)
Had I known I would have
brewed you up some yellow fever-grass
and arsenic

but we were peaceful then
child-like in the yellow dawn of our innocence

so in exchange for a string of islands
and two continents

you gave us a string of beads
and some hawk's bells

which was fine by me personally
for I have never wanted to possess things
I prefer copper anyway
the smell pleases our lord Yucahuna
our mother Attabeira
It's just that copper and gold hammered into guanin
worn in the solar pendants favoured by our holy men
fooled you into thinking we possessed the real thing
(you were not the last to be fooled by our
patina)

As for silver
I find that metal a bit cold
The contents of our mines
I would have let you take for one small mirror
to catch and hold the sun

I like to feel alive
to the possibilities
of yellow

lightning striking

perhaps as you sip tea
at three in the afternoon
a bit incontinent
despite your vast holdings
(though I was gratified to note
that despite the difference in our skins
our piss was exactly the same shade of yellow)

I wished for you
a sudden enlightenment that
we were not the Indies
nor Cathay
No Yellow Peril here
though after you came
plenty of bananas
oranges
sugar cane
You gave us these for our
maize
pineapples
guavas
— in that respect
there was fair exchange

But it was gold
on your mind
gold the light
in your eyes
gold the crown
of the Queen of Spain
(who had a daughter)
gold the prize
of your life
the crowning glory
the gateway to heaven
the golden altar
(which I saw in Seville
five hundred years after)

Though I couldn't help noticing
(this filled me with dread):

silver was your armour
silver the cross of your Lord
silver the steel in your countenance
silver the glint of your sword
silver the bullet I bite

Golden the macca
the weeds
which mark our passing
the only survivors
on yellow-streaked soil

We were The Good Indians
The Red Indians
The Dead Indians

We were not golden
We were a shade too brown.

2

At some hotel
overlooking the sea
you can take tea
at three in the afternoon
served by me
skin burnt black as toast
(for which management apologizes)

but I've been travelling long
cross the sea in the sun-hot
I've been slaving in the cane rows
for your sugar
I've been ripening coffee beans
for your morning break
I've been dallying on the docks
loading your bananas
I've been toiling in orange groves
for your marmalade
I've been peeling ginger
for your relish
I've been chopping cocoa pods
for your chocolate bars
I've been mining aluminium
for your foil

And just when I thought
I could rest
pour my own
– something soothing
like fever-grass and lemon –
cut my ten
in the kitchen
take five

a new set of people
arrive
to lie bare-assed in the sun
wanting gold on their bodies
cane-rows in their hair
with beads — even bells

So I serving them
coffee
tea
cock-soup
rum
Red Stripe beer
sensimilla
I cane-rowing their hair
with my beads

But still they want more
want it strong
want it long
want it black
want it green
want it dread

Though I not quarrelsome
I have to say: look
I tired now

I give you the gold
I give you the land
I give you the breeze
I give you the beaches
I give you the yellow sand
I give you the golden crystals

And I reach to the stage where
(though I not impolite)
I have to say: lump it
or leave it
I can't give anymore

For one day before I die
from five hundred years of servitude
I due to move
from kitchen to front verandah
overlooking the Caribbean Sea
drinking real tea
with honey and lemon
eating bread (lightly toasted, well buttered)
with Seville orange marmalade

I want to feel mellow
in that three o'clock yellow

I want to feel
though you own
the silver tea service
the communion plate
you don't own
the tropics anymore

I want to feel
you cannot take away

the sun dropping by every day
for a chat

I want to feel
you cannot stop
Yellow Macca bursting through
the soil reminding us
of what's buried there

You cannot stop
those street gals
those streggehs
Allamanda
Cassia
Poui
Golden Shower
flaunting themselves everywhere

I want to feel:

you cannot tear my song
from my throat

you cannot erase the memory
of my story

you cannot catch
my rhythm

(for you have to born
with that)

you cannot comprehend
the magic

of anacondas changing into rivers
like the Amazon
boas dancing in my garden
arcing into rainbows
(and I haven't had a drop
to drink – yet)

You cannot reverse
Bob Marley wailing

making me feel
so mellow

in that Caribbean yellow
at three o'clock

any day now.

HURRICANE STORY, 1903

I

Time and time again, Grandmother plucked
bits of fowl coop from the pinguin fence.
Grandfather drained his fields, shored up
their lives against improvidence.
When the earth baked hard again, into
the forest he walked to cut the thatch
to patch his house. Corn drying in the husk
he hung from the rafters while afu yam
and sweet potato ripened (safe from
breeze-blow) underground.

2

When the wind rose in '03, he opened his
tin trunk, took his good clothes out
and packed the corn in. Granny topped it
with cassava bammies and chaklata balls
with a nutmeg and cinnamon leaf tied
with string. After the storm, Granny
would extract milk from fallen coconuts,
make coconut oil to fry the bammies, grate
corn to make porridge, melt the chocolate
in hot milk with cinnamon and nutmeg
to give us courage.

3

In those days storm warning came by
telegraph to Postmistress. Living in
the bush, Grandfather couldn't see her
rush to broadcast the news by posting
a black flag. But he was the seventh son
of a seventh son and could read signs
and interpret wonders so when the swallows
flew below the roof line, when the sky
took on a special peach glow, when flocks
of birds sailed west over the hill,
when clouds banked at the far side and the air
was still, he knew it was time to batten down.
Into the house Granny brought her goat
and fowls – though in the excitement,
two birds fled.

4

Grandfather knew just when to board
the last window up and brace the door.
Noah's Ark was never as crowded and wet.
Thatch blew about and whipped our faces,
water seeped in, but on Grandfather's bed
we rode above it, everything holding
together. For my grandfather had learnt
from his father and his father before him
all the ways of orchestrating disaster.
And my grandmother schooled on Sankeys
led us in singing. In our frail bark
in total darkness we passed through the eye
and out the other side, till all was still.
When Grandfather opened the window the sun
was shining.

Granny hitched up her skirt and petticoats
to unseemly heights (we children had never
seen so much skin). Stood waist deep
in the water in her yard and searched
the blue skies for a sign as Noah's wife did.
She found it when her missing sensay fowl
and favourite leghorn rooster turned up safe
but ruffled, having spent the night together
in the hole in the Cotton Tree.

And as we put our lives back together
I too young to be schooled yet on disaster
spent my time watching that sensay fowl that
strutting leghorn rooster, dying to be
the first to see the strange bird fated
to be born out of that great storm.

MOONSHINE DOLLY

Each full moon

I lay flat on the ground
with outstretched limbs
while you outlined my body
with bits of glass, mirrors
stones.

I would rise
leaving Moonshine Dolly
my ghostly self
behind.

One night
flat on my back
gazing at the full moon's face
I was too scared to rise
for *she* was pulling and pulling –

"Get up," you said,
"You're spoiling the game."

To Moonshine Dolly I whispered: "Hold me tight."

For she was pulling so
and if I rose
you'd run to grab hold
and you'd rise too
and all the children
would come running after
and there we'd be
holding on to each other

leaving far below

Moonshine Dolly
gazing
at this chain of children
rising and rising

to the moon.

HURRICANE STORY, 1944

Each weekday morning
my father the dandy put on
his bicycle clips
his straw boater
and pens lined up in pocket
hair slicked down
vowels well oiled
he rode off to work at
Solomon's Drygoods and Haberdashery
where he was assistant (white-collar class)

Every Sunday
dressed the same way to flaunt his glory
he pedalled uphill for miles
to where his navel-string was buried
and when he left
freewheeling downhill
his barefoot country brothers
ran long distances behind
falling back from exhaustion
while their pride
their hope
kept riding
on that frail back

Then (his mother complained)
before he get establish and
help his own family to gain
their due reward
as is only right and proper
as it ordain (as it set out in the Good Book amen)
he take up with this girl
that don't come from nowhere
she dark she plain

nobody know what
he see in her when
a man his calibre could get
any girl he want (little most)
Mark My Words
she going cause him to turn down
again

But through her
they got the house
for though he was a gentleman in good employment
(first class) it plain to see
(she of few words said)
one body money can't stretch

She turned back to the soil

You see what I mean his mother said
also: you mek yu own bed you must lie on it
and: we all have we own row to hoe

My mother who hardly ever spoke
crooned hymns in the garden
to her skellion tomatis pumpkin melon
which thrived (as everybody knows)
from her constant labouring
(nothing like a pregnant woman to encourage
pumpkin and melon)
she sang mournful hymns as she reaped
sang as she took her crops to market

My father never wanted
a higgler for a wife
never wanted to turn back
to that life he'd escaped from
never wanted (in public)
to acknowledge this rooting
in the soil

But the house must be paid for
(though nothing for insurance)
the children fed
sent to school

In '44 when the hurricane struck
it all came unstuck
the roof the fields the job
(for Mr Solomon lost his shop
and laughingly retired on *his* insurance)

My mother clapped her hands and
ordered us children
to comb the nearby fields
for battered planks
and twisted corrugated zinc
ordered us to climb up
nail the roof back down
ordered us to thank the Lord each night
for what we were about to receive
– black cerasee tea and water crackers –
ordered us early in the morning
to come into the garden before school
to pick caterpillars
off tomatis and melon
ordered us to grow straight
like skellion

My father stopped putting brilliantine
on his hair
his vowels went flat
as the tyres on the bicycle he finally sold
to buy us schoolbooks
he never noticed we had stolen his pens (telltale ink
leaking from our pockets) never noticed
the battered straw boater disappear
(jauntily reappearing on top of our mother's
head-tie as she strode off to market one day)

No job he could find
worthy of a man of his abilities
(his mother agreed)
couldn't turn back to the muck
when his hands had been clean for so long
something bound to turn up

Meantime
he coasted downhill
and we settled into our new routine:
Monday Tuesday Wednesday our mother worked in the fields
Thursday Friday she went to market
Saturday she left him money on the dresser
He took it and went to Unity Bar and Grocery got drunk
came home and beat her
Sunday she went to church and sang

CAT'S CRADLE

Playing
cat's cradle

I could tie
the sun up tight

there'd be no night

but then with endless day
you'd stay out there so far away
playing out your lines

and I'd be here
playing cat's cradle.

Without you

too long
the day

I untie
the sun

You haul in
the night.

CARIBBEAN BASIN INITIATIVE

"The canoes being small . . . the water lapped over
the edge in an alarming way. Had any of us sneezed...
we must have foundered."
   – Mary Kingsley: *Travels in West Africa*, 1897

I

Like limpets we cling
on craft that ply
in these waters
where our dreams lie.

Afraid to draw breath
lest we stir up
the waves, our faces
might crack but no smile
will spill out; a look
can cause listing: we all
look within; we know
to keep still, we are
still in our graves.

2

No sailor am I.
I was farming
till my seed
failed to yield
fell on stony
ground. I cried:

What is harder
than stone?

Never knew
at the time
the answer is:

Water.

3

My mother sought a sign
in the basin.

She said: sky's so clear
nothing's given back here.

I said: Agué Lord of the Sea
rules over me.

You can't keep
a good man down,

if you born to hang
you can't drown.

4

So many passengers
we listed; so much
bailing out as we
drifted, our numbers
kept shrinking and as
the nights passed,
our bodies got lighter
so we were never sinking
as low as some
we never saw rise again
out of that water.

Not all trunks will float.

5

Marcelin and Anselm
unseasoned young men
went into the forest
to cut the tree for
their boat. It's funny
how grudgingly that
tree fell. Funny how
each day it grew back
again. They never could
hollow it enough to
make it float.

Never send a boy to
do a man's job, I say.
They will not follow
the old way.

Feed the spirits before
you feed the children.
Before you make the first
cut, you must pay.

Some rules cannot
be flouted. Some gods
will not uphold
the unconverted.

Agué Lord of the Sea:
Watch over me.

6

After weeks of
dead reckoning
no beckoning
landfall; I hang
by a thread
to my dream.
We were seeking
the Gulf Stream:
it is we who
are found.

Reclaimed,

we are bound
for an island
a stone's throw
from our own.

No mariners here.
Here there be
Marines.

Yes, sir!

7

What is stronger
than stone?

Nothing's stronger
than this cage
on Guantanamo,
nothing's bounded
as this rage
as this basin.

Yes.

Sir!

8

louvri baryè pou mwen

9

They're shipping me home.
I've been spared
to navigate again
some other dry season.

Though we drift
past all sign
past all meaning
past all reason

Though we see
in the basin
white sand
from our bones

Though we thirst
till we die
surrounded
by water

Like limpets we'll cling
on craft that ply
in these waters
where our dreams lie.

HURRICANE STORY, 1951

Margaret and her man Delbert
such a fine young couple
everybody said
so full of ambition
so striving
their little boy so bright
so handsome
so thriving

Though in 1951 after the hurricane
struck they ended up suck-
ing salt same as everybody else

Margaret said: Look
we'll never get anything back together
unless we do something serious
something really ambitious
Plenty people going to England now
plenty women going in for nursing
Let me go
while you continue here
with the farming
Just for the
time being
As soon as I
graduate I'll come back
get big job
That time see me in
mi whites nuh
Soon turn Matron

Together
we can build a good life
for our son

But somehow she never
got far with the nursing
for in her life she never
knew people could hard so
never thought a country could cold so
With her heart turning into stone
with nothing to show for it
— she wanted so much
for the boy — she decided
though she would continue striving
she wouldn't write again
until she could send him
what amounted to
something

The man begging his mother
to keep the boy said: So-so
farming can't take us too far
This can never provide my son
with the life I want for him

He set off for America
to be a farm worker
Every year he went
to pick oranges

Those on his tree
in his yard
turned black from blight
for he never came back
to that piece of ground

He settled in the city
Got married
Sometimes (when prodded)
he sent something
for the boy
He had
other things
on his mind now
He was ambitious
and striving again
Going far

Granny said
to the boy:

Hard-ears children
can't reach nowhere
you will
never amount
to anything

His ears
weren't hard
he was just
hard of hearing
After a while
he also stopped speaking

His granny wrote
to his father (whom
he couldn't remember)
to come and get him
saying:

I old
I can't strive with him
any more

His father saying
he would try with him
came and took him home and
introduced him:

This is your sister Rose
This is your brother Reuben
This is your sister Carol Ann
This is your brother Jonathan
and this is your new mother
Miss Sharon (a lady who looked
as if she had learnt to smile
out of a book)

After a while
they said he was too hard-ears
to amount to anything
and left him alone

He'd go by the shore
and practise writing
(without a pen):

First he blew breath
across the water
"Ah—"

After that
every day
he'd go and call out
Ah
O

Ah–o
Ah–o
Ah–

He threw the sounds across
the ocean like stones hoping
they'd hit
something

rebound off

someone
he couldn't give
a name to

but only by an echo
returning
would he know:
the ocean wasn't as empty
as he was

Every day now

Ah–o
Ah–o
Ah

Till one day
he managed:

Ah–o
Ah–o
Ma–

Soon the sounds
would make syllables
the syllables
would make words
the words
would make phrases
the phrases
would make poems

His mother
would never read them
she was too busy
swabbing out
a hospital
in Reading
England

After so many years
she no longer even
thought of him
(or anything else
for that matter)
gazing
day after day
into
that
pail
of water

Until
one day
as she sluiced out
a ward
she fancied she heard
someone
calling her name

Ma—

It sounded as if
it came
from the
pail
it sounded like
her rightful name
(not the name
– Miss Black –
by which she
was known here)
No one here
knew *that* name

Ah–o
Ah–o
Ma—

Each day
she poured
more and more
water
on the floor
to try to
capture
that sound

Miss Black
Matron said
(finally)
this just
won't do

No she said
turning the taps
on full
flooding
the ward
pouring out
an ocean
from her pail

Standing
by that shore
she clearly heard
her name now

Ma−

I must go she said
taking off her shoes

I must go now
taking off her overalls

I must go to my −
stripping off her clothes

− son

in Aenon Town, Jamaica −

stepping into
the water
(as they rushed
to restrain her)

− my son
my s −

Standing on that far shore
he heard at last rebound
the sound he'd sent
though slightly bent
by distance

and without conscious intent
he started walking

to meet it

ILLEGAL IMMIGRANT

If I never make this uncharted
                    passage
one way or another, never tell
                    my children
their insolvent eyes set me
                    sailing.
To reach, no ocean's too wide
                    for the leap
no depths too deep to be
                    plumbed
no body too shiftless to fit
                    this dugout.

STOWAWAY

There's this much space between me and
        discovery
a hairline fracture getting wider with
        each wave.
I feel it, though I cannot see to
        hold
my thoughts together – they're
        running loose
all over; someone's bound
        to trip,
I know it. One day light will enter
        this grave.
Till then, I let my thoughts go.
        Dangerously
unstrung, I dive deeper into this
        fault, this
undeclared passage. Without soundings
        there's no telling
how unfathomable the fall, how
        attainable
the littoral. Surfacing
        I'll dangle
on a single hope: that my eyes
        be blinded
only by the promised land.

MEDITATION ON RED

"I feel I've been here for . . . centuries. Even this
winter dates from the dark ages."
– Jean Rhys, letter from Cheriton Fitzpaine, Devon

I

You, voyager
in the dark
landlocked
at Land Boat Bungalows no. 6
never saw this
green
wide
as the sea
green
limitless
as the rain
that greeted your arrival
at Cheriton Fitzpaine.

You (destiny:
storm-tossed)
never saw
the rolling downs
patchworked
in emerald, peridot
mint, celadon
never saw
sheep
tossed here and there
like foam
for decoration

on this green
quilt
of Devon.

Arrival
at Land Boat Bungalows
at flood time
never rid you of
the fear of being
the fear of being left
the fear of being left
          high and dry

So at no. 6
there was
perpetual flooding
so much drink
flowing
so much tears
so much
on the edge of
but never quite
under
that quilted
green
comforter
wishing for
blue skies
wanting
but never quite
believing
your craft
to be
worthy.

Such
disappointing
harbour
(again).

"It is very cold," you write
"It gets dark early.
One meets dark figures . . .
frost and ice are everywhere."

You still had
this burning
desire
to set sail
even though
(now and always)
and despite
what long ago
the fortune teller
said –
"I see something great
in your hand, something noble" –
you were
rudderless.

Marooned
in the grey
you decided
to garden.

Since
they called you
witch
you would
conjure up
bright

flowers
spelling
each other
all year.

In spring
(you wrote)
you planted seeds.
"I wanted heaps of poppies . . .

Not one came up."

Instead
(you wrote)
there was sometimes
"blue murder
in my wicked heart"

and a red dress
in your closet
a "Christmas cracker dress"
– the whole village knew and whispered
waiting for another explosion

(like that
which long ago
came
from the
attic).

But you
in your housecoat
frayed
round the edges
like you
red

like your rages
(soothed
with a box
of pills, red
what else?)
found
there were
occasional
red-letter days:
a dream of red
and gilt
a dream of
getting your face
lifted
buying
a bright red wig
to shock
and a purple dress
with pearls
to hoist
your spirits
(when you voyaged
out).

Meantime each day
you made up
your old face
carefully
for the village
children
making faces
at you
who knew
how to spell

little knowing
in that grey mist
hanging over
Cheriton Fitzpaine
how cunningly
you masked
your pain
how carefully
you honed
your craft
how tightly
you held
your pen
how brilliantly
you planned
to write
(though they
no doubt
heard it
as "ride")
across that
Wide Sargasso.

2

Now in the time
of that incredible green
again
in spring
in rain
I come
to the churchyard
at Cheriton Fitzpaine
Devon

knowing
you're there
Lady
sleeping it off
under that dark
grey
stone
though it says
in a categorical
tone:

HERE LIE BURIED THE ASHES
OF MY BELOVED MOTHER
JEAN RHYS, C.B.E., NOVELIST
(ELLA GWENDOLEN HAMER)
BORN
DOMINICA AUGUST 24TH 1890
DIED
EXETER MAY 14TH 1979.

"GOOD MORNING MIDNIGHT."

I've come to
wake you
with spring flowers
(the ones
you had no
luck with
growing)
– snowdrops
daffodils
narcissus

knowing
you would prefer
a blanket

of red
– flame of the forest
hibiscus
heliconia
poinsettia
firecracker
bougainvillea –

for of
Mr Rochester's
first wife
you said:

"She is cold
– and fire
is the only warmth
she knows
in England."

I apologize.

Right now
I'm as divided
as you were
by that sea.

But I'll
be able to
find my way
home again

for that craft
you launched
is so seaworthy
tighter
than you'd ever been

dark voyagers
like me
can feel free
to sail.

That fire
you lit
our beacon
to safe harbour
in the islands.

I'd like to take
with me
a picture

and though
you were never one
for photographs
or symmetry
(except
in fiction)
it's to be taken
by the woman
who typed
your last
book.

And though
I know you hate
to be disturbed
just
when you've finally
settled
down
I beg you
to tear yourself

away
from that grey stone
in the churchyard
at Cheriton Fitzpaine
for just one moment
and –

Look,
Miss Rhys:

No rain!

– and see
Mary Stephenson
standing there
at her ease
waiting
to say
to us both:

"Smile please."

HURRICANE STORY, 1988

My mother wasn't christened
Imelda but she stashed a cache
of shoes beneath the bed.

She used to travel to Haiti,
Panama, Curaçao, Miami,
wherever there was bargain

to catch – even shoes that
didn't have match. Back home
she could always find customer

come bend-down to look and talk
where she plant herself on
sidewalk. When the hurricane

hit, she ban her belly and bawl,
for five flights a day to Miami
grounded. No sale and her shoes

getting junjo from the damp (since
the roof decamp) and the rest
sitting in Customs, impounded.

My mother banked between her
breasts, lived out her dreams
in a spliff or two each night.

Since the storm, things so tight
her breasts shrivel, the notes
shrinking. Every night she there

thinking. Every morning she get up
and she wail: Lawd! Life so soak-up
and no bail out. To raatid!

ALL CLEAR, 1928

I was beating chaklata when someone
came shouting: A stranger man come!

I dropped everything. Same way
in my sampata, my house dress,

my everyday head-tie, I rushed to
the square wondering: could it be?

How many gathered there so long
after our men disappeared into

the black water dividing us from
Puerto Limón, Havana, Colón

knew it was he? Not his sons lost
to a father fifteen years gone.

There he was. Leather-booted and
spurred, sitting high on a fine horse.

Never spoke a word. This Spanish
grandee sat on his horse and

looked at us. Looked through us.
Never could lump poverty. Used

to say: Esmie, when I strike it rich
in foreign what a fine gentleman

I'll be. And you with your clear
complexion will sit beside me,

your hands stilled from work
like silk again (silk of my skin

my only dowry!) Ashamed now of my
darkened complexion, my work-blackened

hands, my greying hair, a loosening
of my pride (three sons with Mr Hall

the carpenter who took me in) I
lowered my eyes and tried to hide.

I needn't have bothered. He looked
so troubled, as if he'd lost his way.

And suddenly, with nothing said,
he wheeled his horse and fled.

And ever after we talked of the
wonder of it. The stranger never

spoke to anyone. Forgotten the young
man who left home with a good white

shirt (stitched by these hands) and
a borrowed black serge suit (which

the owner never recovered), a heng-pon-me
with four days ration of roasted salt fish,

johnny cakes, dokunu and cerasee for tea
to tide him over to the SS *Atrato*

lying in wait in Kingston Harbour.
All, all the men went with our dreams,

our hopes, our prayers. And he
with a guinea from Mass Dolphy

the schoolteacher who said that boy
had so much ambition he was bound

to go far. And he had. Gathering
to himself worlds of experience

which allowed him to ride over us
with a clear conscience. I never

told anyone. For I would have had
to tell his children why he hadn't

sent money for bread, why his fine
leather boots, why his saddle,

his grey mare, his three-piece suit,
his bowler hat, his diamond tie-pin,

his fine manicured hands, his barbered
hair, his supercilious air. Never

was a more finely-cut gentleman
seen in our square. And I trembled

in anger and shame for the black limbo
into which my life had fallen

all these years till my hands touched
the coarse heads of my young sons

recalling me to a snug house clad
with love. And I cried then, because

till he came back I had not known
my life was rooted. Years later,

I learned that his fine gentlemanly air,
his polished boots, manners, and Ecuador

gold bought him a very young girl of very
good family in Kingston. And they wed.

He, with a clear conscience.
She, with a clear complexion.

NATURE STUDIES

PLANTS

Plants are deceptive. You see them there
looking as if once rooted they know
their places; not like animals, like us
always running around, leaving traces.

Yet from the way they breed (excuse me!)
and twine, from their exhibitionist
and rather prolific nature, we must infer
a sinister not to say imperialistic

grand design. Perhaps you've regarded,
as beneath your notice, armies of mangrove
on the march, roots in the air, clinging
tendrils anchoring themselves everywhere?

The world is full of shoots bent on conquest,
invasive seedlings seeking wide open spaces,
matériel gathered for explosive dispersal
in capsules and seed cases.

Maybe you haven't quite taken in the
colonizing ambitions of hitchhiking
burrs on your sweater, surf-riding nuts
bobbing on ocean, parachuting seeds and other

airborne traffic dropping in. And what
about those special agents called flowers?
Dressed, perfumed, and made-up for romancing
insects, bats, birds, bees, even you –

– don't deny it, my dear, I've seen you
sniff and exclaim. Believe me, Innocent,
that sweet fruit, that berry, is nothing
more than ovary, the instrument to seduce

you into scattering plant progeny. Part of
a vast cosmic program that once set
in motion cannot be undone though we
become plant food and earth wind down.

They'll outlast us, they were always there
one step ahead of us: plants gone to seed,
generating the original profligate,
extravagant, reckless, improvident, weed.

STARAPPLE

Expect no windfall here.
Don't stand and wait
    at this portal between
shadow and light.
Two-sided starapple leaf
    can't be trusted as guide.
Without force, starapple
    won't let go of its fruit.
Too afraid you'll discover
    the star already fallen
    the apple compromised.

PINEAPPLE

With *yayama*
fruit of the Antilles,
we welcomed you
to our shores,
not knowing in
your language
"house warming"
meant "to take
possession of"
and "host"
could so easily
turn hostage.

Oblivious
of irony,
you now claim
our symbol
of hospitality
as your own,
never suspecting
the retribution
incarnate
in that sweet
flesh.

So you
plant pineapples
arrayed in fields
like battalions
not knowing
each headdress
of spikes
is slanted
to harness
the sun's
explosions

and store them
within
the fruit's
thick skin
on which
– unless
you can peel
them off quick –
pineal eyes
watch and
wait,
counting
down.

MADAM FATE

When
Lucifer
fell
he landed
on our pasture.
He rose again
posing
as innocent
star-flower.
Penetrating
his new guise
we recognize
notorious
Madam Fate,
her poison
as potent
as his
last
drop.

FERN

1

Fern inherent
in this spore
uncoils
the green leaf
into light
on branch's
brown
recoil.

2

Fern was present
at Creation fired
the carbon of
revolution fuelled
the age of industry
in which inheres
its diminution.

MOUNTAIN PRIDE

Like Mountain Pride
every September
I go hurtling off cliffs
    hurtling off cliffs

again.

SUN AND MOON

Moon's
desire
to play
with
fire

caused
Sun
to run.

Let's
pray
they
stay
that
way.

SNAIL

O snail
so slow
so low
we can hardly
stoop
far enough
to see
outlined
behind
what might be
the cosmic
trail.

GUAVA

Than guava fruit
nothing sweeter
so free in its wild simplicity
so generous
it makes itself available to all comers
– even the worms.

GUAVA/2
(for Myrth)

Maud was making guava jelly
when she said to me: "I don't
like it when guava tree starts
to bear too much. I take it
as a sign. Remember that time
in Barbados?"

. . . that house scented with guava
and Maud trying to reduce the vast
quantity of fruit you kept harvesting.
That week she made guava jelly, guava
cheese, guava paste, stewed guava,
and blended the pulp into drink.
But your tree would not stop
producing. It bore faster than she
could cook or we could consume.

I think of you, stricken so suddenly.
I say nothing. To her it would seem
extreme if I said that the Taino
zemi of the dead is called Maquetaurie
Guayaba – Lord of the Guava – and that
it is he who instructs the tree when
to speed up production so that
the incoming soul will have enough of
the fragrance of guava to feed on.

GUINEP

Our mothers have a thing
about guinep:

Mind you don't eat guinep in your good clothes.
It will stain them.

Mind you don't climb guinep tree.
You will fall.

Mind you don't swallow guinep seed.
It will grow inside you.

Our mothers have a thing
about guinep: they're
secretly consuming it.

ANATTO AND GUINEP

No one today regards anatto and guinep
as anything special.

No one puts them on stamps or
chooses them

for praise-songs or any kind
of festival.

Country people one time used anatto
to colour their food,

these days you can hardly get it
not even at the market.

As for guinep: that's worse. Big people
scorn it

(though they eat it). Only children confess
they love it.

Well, with the Arawaks and others who were
here before us

it wasn't so. Nothing could happen without
anatto paste

or guinep stain to paint their bodies
with.

Guinep black to summon the rain clouds;
anatto red

for war. They also used both for things
in between like

medicine and curing or birth or death.
Patterns in red

or black were to them like dressing up
for occasions.

They wore these colours on their bodies
as we wear clothes:

to protect themselves, to signify or
engage in play,

as markers on the road of life or as
flags signalling

in the most straightforward way:
look at me:

I'm beautiful! So give a thought to
forgotten anatto

to humble guinep and the memory
of the ol'people

who weren't the first to wear them
anyway:

How do you think Moon got stained
black like that?

What do you think Sun used to redden
its face?

PAWPAW

Everybody likes pawpaw
but some don't like it planted
too near the house.

Me too.

I know for a fact
that tree will sap your strength
waste your muscle
draw you down
to skin and bone.
To nutten.
An ol'lady
told me that.

It's better to plant it
the far side of the fence.

You can laugh
and call it superstitious
nonsense
but if you want proof
just wrap pawpaw leaf
round a tough piece of beef
or mutton
and wait
and see
if it don't draw it down
to nutten.

Just like the ol'lady did say.

BAMBOO
(In Five Variations)

I

"Bamboo love" burns
bright and hot
and comes (and goes)
in flashes

leaving behind
as residue
fugitive
bamboo ashes.

2

Bamboo prides itself on knowing
the art of living long:

before wind, rain, axe and forager
humbly bending

while secretly sending deep into
cliff or mire

roots that are grasping and strong,
to spread. Not always

as quickly as that dread enemy
of conceit: fire.

3

If Stone had been a better debater,
Man (like Stone) would be living
forever. But long ago when such
matters were settled, Stone lost
the argument for eternity to Bamboo.
The clincher came with Bamboo saying:
it's true, this way Man will die,
like me. But look along this endless
river-bank, what do you see? So Man
could be. With careful tending,
despite my periodic ending, from
my roots young shoots spring, routinely.

4

Cows grazing on fresh bamboo shoot
gaze at eleven-year-old me lying at
bamboo root, in my sanctuary: dried bamboo
leaves my bed, my head buried in a book.

"The Little Prodigy," my Great-Aunt
Emily (sarcastically) calls me when
I refuse to help her dust or cook,
polish silver or learn to use a hook

to fish up thread or wool in her tortures
called crochet and knitting. To keep her
from having further fit in my idle
presence, at my earliest convenience

I take off over the picket fence, across
the pasture to lie in that dense bamboo
thicket. All who pass by call out to
remind me that Duppies inhabit bamboo root

and if I don't take care those spirits
will cause my head to twist around, my
tongue to tie, my eyes to shoot up
straight out of my head as bamboos do

from the ground. Still, as often as
possible I perversely choose to lie and
court fright on dry leaves that rustle,
under bamboo joints that creak, troubled

only by the thought that Great-Aunt Emily
would experience such delight if a Duppy
(or the cat) actually got my tongue.
"A nice kind of heathen we're raising"

she says talking over my head to some
invisible presence Up There (for such
weighty matters to me cannot be
directly communicated). And only because

I said Church Makes Me Sneeze (which is
true). In view of her great age and to
avoid further outrage I bite my tongue
and wisely don't say that if she would only

leave me alone, one day in bamboo cathedral
I might encounter even the Holy Spirit,
for there I find I can breathe in (without
sneezing) a naturally fresh and liberating air.

5

You say you've been to my house
in the hills and never heard
from my high window

something like a dry rustle
from the river-bank, a long blue
sighing? Yes, maybe (as you say)

it wasn't the wind dying
in bamboo leaves and yes maybe
that isn't the sound of wild

bamboo flutes scaling up and down
mountain passes which I keep
hearing from this high window

near St. Clair Avenue Toronto
Canada which is not where
river-bank or hill is.

GARDENING IN THE TROPICS

BRIEF LIVES

Gardening in the Tropics, you never know
what you'll turn up. Quite often, bones.
In some places they say when volcanoes
erupt, they spew out dense and monumental
as stones the skulls of *desaparecidos*
– the disappeared ones. Mine is only
a kitchen garden so I unearth just
occasional skeletons. The latest
was of a young man from the country who
lost his way and crossed the invisible
boundary into rival political territory.
I buried him again so he can carry on
growing. Our cemeteries are thriving too.
The newest addition was the drug baron
wiped out in territorial competition
who had this stunning funeral
complete with twenty-one-gun salute
and attended by everyone, especially
the young girls famed for the vivacity
of their dress, their short skirts and
even briefer lives.

MY FATHER'S BLUE PLANTATION

Gardening in the Tropics we revel in
Hot Tropical Colours. My father's land
was blue. In his prime, his banana
plantation came right to our doorstep.
We lived deep in this forest of leaves
made blue by the treatment against
Leaf Spot Disease which he humped around
the fields in a battered spray-pan. On
Banana Day (which I think was Wednesday)
we went off to school eyeing all the way
the bunches wrapped in blue banana-trash
waiting at the roadside for the truck.
We fervently prayed ours would find
acceptance in the sight of the Inspector
for every bunch was earmarked to pay for
something. Sometimes it was shoes. We
didn't choose those in Hot Tropical Colours
since each child could have only one pair
(for school and chapel) and we were taught
only black or white would find favour
in His sight.

But all this was ages ago.
We children fled the blue for northern
light where we buy up all the shoes
in sight. My closet is filled – finally –
with a rainbow of shoes in Hot Tropical
Colours (which look marvellous against
the snow). My father's house (I'm told)
is visible from all directions now
(some crops grow only in young gardens).
Alone, fanning sand and stoning breeze,
my father lets in all that air, lets that
Hot Tropical Sun pour down to fill his
blue lungs and warm his old and vegetating
bones.

FINDING YOUR STONE

Gardening in the Tropics
you never know what you'll
turn up. Yesterday it was bones,
today: stones. Here's one
that might be holy. To test,
tie white cotton thread
around it. Hold over a flame.
If the thread doesn't burn
you've found it: a power stone.
Breathe lightly on it to confirm.
You see it sweating? Even the gods
perspire. Take your *pierre* home
and feed it. The heart gets weak
if the spirit is kept
too dry.

THE KNOT GARDEN

Gardening in the Tropics,
you'll find things that don't
belong together often intertwine
all mixed up in this amazing fecundity.
We grow as convoluted as the vine.
Or wis. And just as quickly!
Only last week as our leader left
for another IMF meeting, he ordered
the hacking out of paths and
ditches, the cutting of swaths
to separate out flowers
from weeds, woods from trees. But
somebody (as usual) didn't get it
right (what goes on in mixed
farming is actually quite hard
to envision since so many things
propagate underground, by
division). Returning, our leader
finds instead of neat trench
and barricade separating species,
higglers and drug barons moving
into the more salubrious climes
while daughters of gentry are
crossing lines to sleep with
ghetto boys with gold teeth
and pockets full of dollars
derived from songs on the hit
parade. In the old days, he'd
have ordered some hits himself
but agencies that give aid
are talking human rights now.
Instead, something more subtle
– like poisoned flour or raging
tenement fires – is allowed

to spread. While citizens are
dying our leader is flying again,
off to another IMF meeting
in the presidential jet high
above this dense tropical jungle.
Meanwhile, the fertilized soil
(nothing like fire to do it)
bursts into new and twisted growth
of such profusion by the time
he returns, it proves
too impenetrable for landing.
Avoiding confusion, our leader
travels on, searching for
unencumbered skies, over the
Cayman Islands, or Liechtenstein,
or Geneva.

THE COLOURS OF BIRDS

Gardening in the Tropics, part of the ambience
derives from the presence of Rare Tropical Birds.

I like it when the parakeets come calling; they
never fail to amuse and entertain. Did you know

it was because of their antics that the Great
Anaconda Monster was finally slain? They made him

laugh – and in so doing expose his tongue – which
the hummingbird (according to plan) pulled out

by the root; the other birds then set to and
killed him for in his skin, his blood, his viscera

and his tongue, the monster had kept for himself
all the colours of the sun. Till that deed was done,

all birds were colourless. After the killing, they dipped
their bodies, legs, heads, and beaks into the palette

of Anaconda's remains to stain themselves with.
Some are such show-offs now, you'd never believe

they came from such tame stock – those families like
the Macaws, the Hummingbirds, the Parrots, and

others I could name and that in any case in the colour
domain the spirit of the Anaconda – as the Rainbow –

continues to reign pre-eminent. But to get back
to the deed. The silly little parakeets just kept on

dancing, making faces and laughing fit to kill so that
by the time they came to their senses it was done

and the other birds had taken their fill, daubing
themselves with every tint under the sun except that

vibrant green which the (now) brilliant wits said was
startling, yes, but too incredibly jejune if made

a whole suit of. To their yellows, blues, and reds
they touched just a smidgen so quite a bit was left back

(which is a good thing for parakeets travel in enormous
packs) and they had to be content with that. They

were not (so they tell), they were so irritated
they squabbled and yelled and threw paint and daubed

at one another till each got deeply saturated with this
vivacious green colour – the exact shade of young

maize (which is why to this day parakeets attack
fields of it since they assume those stationary

birds are mimicking them). In the evenings when
they're flying home I hear them noisily complaining,

still blaming each other for their (almost)
monochromatic lot. Which is why the old ones (for

moral edification and with malicious intent) love
to tell a story about humans: the tale of the

would-be beauty queen who sits in the asylum forever
trying to wash off her skin the stain from those

tropical impurities showing through, that made her
a darker hue than the winner. Poor thing (the

malicious gossips sing), she still hasn't learnt
that throughout our tropical domain, people may all

look different but, unlike the birds, so proud of
their assorted strain and their varicoloured plumage,

that other monster has not yet been slain. So when it
comes to the colour of skin, pigmentation is not yet in.

THE TREE OF LIFE

Gardening in the Tropics was easiest
before the Flood. We had just one tree
to care for – the firstborn, the Tree
of Life. When (after the Great Fire)
the earth was bare and we were starving,
The Mighty One took pity and planted
deep in the interior a tree so
ubiquitous it bore on its branches
food of every different kind. Mapuri
the wild pig discovered it but kept it
hidden, sneaking off behind our backs
to eat his fill. But we suspected
something so we sent our most
skilled detectives to make him spill it.
First, Woodpecker, but he couldn't help
stopping to tap at every charred stump
– which alerted Mapuri to our plan;
others tried, but it was Rat
who succeeded. Of course, Rat being
rat, he tried to keep it hidden too,
but crumbs on his whiskers betrayed him.
We had to threaten to kill him before he
took us there. In front of this
unimaginable tree we fell down and
praised Him – and then we ate our fill.
After that, we merely had to reach
overhead to pluck a nice juicy starapple,
then perhaps a naseberry or two
before gathering for cooking fresh ears
of corn, hot peppers and tomatoes
for seasoning, cassava to make bread
and drink for celebrating.
So imagine our dismay when out of
the blue His voice came one day and said:

Cut the Tree Down! We trembled, but obeyed,
chopping away for generations
until it swayed and fell (water already
starting to trickle from the hole left
by its root – but that is the start of
another tale). He ordered us to take from
the branches slips and cuttings and plant
them everywhere. And that is how we
acquired crops for cultivating. From
that time, I've been a convert of
mixed farming though, of late, I've
noticed the agricultural officers
(those long-sleeved white-shirt boys)
have been coming around to try and
persuade us to chop everything down
and plant only one crop. They say we can
get more money that way – from exporting.
But it's only the young ones they fool.
It's true they're all driving fancy cars
now, they have tractors, big houses,
are sending children to school. But let
them wait till drought or blight
comes round. What will they eat?
You see me here? I'm sticking to the plan
of having all my food, my seasonings and
medicines mixed up in one ground. For if
He wanted us to plant just one thing
in the garden, why did He make us chop
The Tree of Life down?

SEEING THE LIGHT

1

Gardening in the Tropics nowadays means
letting in light: they've brought in machines
that can lay waste hundreds of hectares
in one day, they've brought in (since we have
already passed this way) other peoples to hack
and burn through; smoke obscures the sun for
months now, there are not enough trees to pull down
the rain. The animals are gone too; without hunters
they're no longer game. By the time they've cut
the last tree in the jungle only our bones
will remain as testament to this effort to bring
light (though in their chronicles they might have
recorded it by another name: *Conquista?*
Evangelismo? Civilización?)

2

Before you came, it was dark in our garden,
that's true. We cleared just enough for our huts
and our pathways, opened a pinpoint in the canopy
to let the sun through. We made the tiniest scratch
on Mother Earth (begging her pardon). When we moved
on, the jungle easily closed over that scar again.
We never took more than we needed. Always gave back
(to Earth) our thanks and our praises, never failed
to salute the gods of the rain, the wind, the sun,
and the moon in her phases. Never failed to provide
tobacco smoke for the spirits to feed on that show us
the game. When the yuca or the maize was ripe,
we celebrated. By the stars and planets across
the green (and dark) terrain, we navigated.
In all of this, we took up so little space,

it would have been easy for you to greet us
when you came – and move on. There was enough
in the jungle to provide gardens for everyone.
All over these green and tropical lands there
could have been pinpricks of light filtering
through the leaves to mirror the stars of Heaven,
invert the Pleiades.

3

But from the start, Earth did not please. You
set it alight, you disemboweled it, you forcefully
established marks of your presence all over it.
As you tore up what sustained us, our world
under your sway fell into the true darkness
of Night, fell apart from lack of regulation.
For we no longer had power to summon the spirits
with tobacco, with invocations to harness the
blessings of the sun, the rain. You told us your
one God had the power to bring us the true light,
but we've waited in vain. To this day – as catastrophe
holds sway and earth continues to burn – there are
things we still cannot learn. Why did those
who speak of Light wear black, the colour
of mourning? Why was their countenance so grave?
Why on a dead tree did they nail the bringer
of light, one Cristo, torture and kill him
then ask us to come, bow down and worship him?
Yet, with all the strange things that have happened
to us since your first coming, it's not so hard perhaps
to believe that in some far-off land this Cristo,
this person who had never heard of us, was
nevertheless put to death, gave up his life,
in order to enlighten us. Maybe many more trees
must die to illuminate his death, as many leaves
must fall to cover up our dying.

AMAZON WOMEN

Gardening in the Tropics, sometimes
you come across these strong Amazon
women striding across our lands –
like Toeyza who founded the Wori-
shiana nation of female warriors
in the mountains of Parima – of whom
the missionary Brett and Sir Walter
Raleigh wrote. Though nobody believed
them, I myself could tell a tale or two
(though nothing as exotic as the story
of Toeyza and her lover Walyarima who
swam the river disguised as a black
jaguar whenever he visited her). Now
we've got that out of the way let me
hasten to say I'm not into sensationalism,
I merely wished to set the record
straight by averring that the story
of Amazon women might have begun
because when the warriors went away
– to war or voyages – it was the
women who kept the gardens going
and sometimes if the men were not
heard from again (as occasionally
happened) they banded together and
took up arms to defend the territory.
So somebody – like Cristobal Colón
or Sir Walter Raleigh – could have
come along and heard these (marvellous)
tales of (fabulous) lands full of
(pure) gold and fierce (untamed,
exotic) women (you know how men stay!).
And the rest (as they say) is history.
Mark you, the part about Toeyza's
husband sending her and the other

women to gather cassava for a feast
while he ambushed and killed her lover
is true (at least, my auntie says so
and her husband's uncle's grandfather
told him as a fact – and he got it
from someone who knew). I don't know
about you but the part I find
disgusting is that while they were
away, the husband (a chief at that)
skinned and hung the lover up
in the women's hut as a lesson
to faithless wives. (Though if men
go around in jaguar disguise, what
can they expect?) If you ask me,
that husband got what was coming
(poisoned with bitter cassava juice
mixed in with the beer) though
I can't see what the rest of the men
did to deserve equal treatment.
But that Toeyza (with liberated words)
led all the wives in flight and they
managed (despite pursuit) to fight
their way across the jungle to the
heights and freedom in their own
nation which ever since has been
justly celebrated as the Land of
the Amazon. The best part (I hear)
is that they allow men to visit them
once a year. Boy children they send
back to the land of their fathers,
girls they keep to rear (though
I'm not sure I would want my girl
raised by a band of women outlaws
keeping company with jaguars). But
you see my trial! I'm here gossiping
about things I never meant to air

for nobody could say I'm into
scandal. I wanted to tell of noble women
like Nanny the Maroon queen mother
or the fair Anacaona, Taino
chieftainess who was brutally
slain by the colonists, or of
the Carib women whom the said Colón
relied on for navigation
through the islands. I hadn't meant
to tell tall tale or repeat exotic
story for that's not my style.
But we all have to make a living
and there's no gain in telling stories
about ordinary men and women.
Then again, when gardening
in the Tropics, every time you lift
your eyes from the ground
you see sights that strain your
credulity – like those strong
Amazon women striding daily across
our lands carrying bundles of wood
on their heads and babies strapped
to their breasts and calabashes of
water in both hands.

TROPIC LOVE

Gardening in the Tropics you hear poetry
in some unexpected places. Sitting on my
verandah last night I overheard two people
passing by. The woman said:

> You don't bring me flowers anymore
> – or anything for the children.
> My heart has turned to stone
> but I cannot put that in the pot.
> Love me and my family or leave me
> to sit by the roadside to sell,
> by the riverside taking in washing,
> by milady's fire cooking for my living.
> I'm a woman with heavy responsibilities.
> With my lot I'm prepared to be contented.
> With your sweet words, Lover, tempt me
> not, if you've come empty-handed.

THE IMMOVABLE TENANT

Gardening in the Tropics, sometimes
you come across the most unreasonable
people. Like some tenants (who are

in exactly the same position as me,
it's just that some of us don't
quibble; we accept our lot and cope).

Next door, there's this lady, old as
Methuselah. You'd think she'd yearn
for peace and quiet now since

in her lifetime she's experienced
nothing but upheaval and a succession
of husbands, each one claiming

to be lord of the manor, each
fading from the scene leaving her
as lonesome queen or bereft first lady.

That's because, although they all
liked to pretend they were of enormous
net worth, having title to prove it,

everyone in this area is mortgaged
to the limit to landlords up north
– or bankers across the sea.

And, as my old daddy used to say,
he who pays the piper calls the tune,
or, he who wields the big stick

gives the lick. In my neighbour's
case it's a former husband's uncle
who's as cantankerous as they come

– and rich as Croesus – and as dumb.
Well, perhaps not quite, for he
managed to acquire all that property.

Now he has to go out of his way
to defend it, feeling it gives him
a right to interfere in the business

of all his neighbours to ensure
that none falls prey to other
foreigners and sells out for nothing

(as the old lady's husbands did
– to him). It's no joke, for once
or twice when a few of us in the area

started talking to potential investors
about new types of development for
our holdings, the man turned nasty,

introduced strong-arm tactics, and,
worse, threatened to cut off our access.
That's serious, for while we were

composing calypsos, dancing sambas,
and generally fooling around, he was
out there buying up not just all our

ground, but the very air we breathe;
he's rented our air spaces, taken
control of our seas and beaches;

underground he's taken mining leases
and overhead he's set up satellite dishes.
We all live in dread that we can't

mash ants without his knowing. On top
of it all, he's acquired rights (from
God knows where) to dump (if he wishes)

his garbage on our shores. You see me
here? I'm not lying: when I was younger,
I joined in some protests, gave him

a little scare. I'm not boasting but
maybe a bomb or two had my signature on it,
as did petitions. But that was before

I came to hold him dear. If you play
ball, he'll treat you fair, throw things
your way, include you in the game.

I tell my people now to cool it. For
I've been paid to see the wisdom of
supping with the enemy especially if

he has the longest spoon, the biggest stick,
the deepest pocket. Seeing as how
we're such good buddies now, he's

asked me as a favour to talk to my
neighbour for she's messing up his plans
for that property. He's spent a lot

of money fixing up the place. He wants
to attract tourists, investors and
extractors, for the garden is full of

trees ripe for felling and the house
of treasure priced for selling and there
are minerals to be mined. Everything

is on time, all the necessaries (with
my help) have been dealt with, the right
palms greased, contracts signed.

It's just this miserable old lady living
(on borrowed time) in the basement now
– though he's fixed it up fine. She's

constantly undermining him, screaming
at his tenants and everyone within
hearing (even over his airwaves): "Beware!"

Then she wraps her head in red, puts on
her mourning garments and stalks the
streets disguised as the dread Warner

Woman calling out "Fire! Blood! Repent!"
It's making the tourists and investors
jittery and since it might cause them

to move to a more inviting continent,
she's spoiling it for all of us here,
for people up north (except for Uncle)

can't distinguish one place from an-
other in this hemisphere. What annoys me
is, that old woman is not as mad

as she pretends. My advice would be
to evict her forcibly (precedents
having been set with her husbands

and other malcontents). I'm sure
most of the neighbours would assist
for Uncle has been generous with arms

for self-defence. Though a few
(down the road on the left-hand side)
can be counted on to encourage

her rebellious pride, in the final analysis,
we shall overcome, for we have might
– and right – on our side. It's just that

something about the old woman (which
I can't put my finger on) disturbs me.
When last I met with her, I left her

ranting (as usual) about Uncle tearing
down the old places and rebuilding with
(she says) unseasoned lumber and other

inferior material. She cites this as
another example of environmental
betrayal (for, despite her age, she's up

on whatever topic is the rage). She
claims that her father, after cutting
timber, waited centuries for it to render

all that stored up water before using it
for building. That way, the occupants
might have come and gone but

the structure lived on. She says these
hurry-come-up schemers build on sand.
She's watching them fill up their pockets

but she knows once the going gets rough,
the digging too tough, they'll leave,
abandon her house and land, jettison

their efforts to the jungle. As soon as
they spy next door the fabulous new
virgin territory – they'll move on.

To add to my discomfiture, each time
I'm leaving, that crazy lady croons:
Strangers might occupy my house and land

from time to time, but from this redoubt,
I always repossess it, inch by inch.
With the help of the steadfast tropical

sun, wind, and rain, with the help of the
termites, the ants, the wood lice, and
the worms, I always reclaim. I can wait,

unforgiving. Unlike the rest of you
who slaughter time, I've learnt the art
of eking out my living.

GARDENING ON THE RUN

I

Gardening in the Tropics for us
meant a plot hatched quickly,
hidden deep in forest or jungle,
run to ground behind palisade or
palenque, found in cockpit, in
quilombo or *cumbe*. In Hispaniola,
where they first brought me
in 1502 in Ovando's fleet,
as soon as we landed I absconded
and took to the forest. Alone,
I fell in with runaways who
didn't look like me though
(I took this as a sign) their
bodies were stained black (with
grey markings) – in mourning
they said, for the loss of their
homeland, else they would have
been painted red. The bakras
called them wild Indians, me they
called runaway, maroon, cimarron.
No matter what they called, I
never answered. As fast as they
established plantations and brought
millions like me across the sea,
in chains, to these lands, the
dread of mutilation, starvation,
transportation, or whip, counted
less than the fear of life
under duress in the Americas.
The brave ones abandoned plantation
for hinterland, including women
with children and others waiting

to be born right there in the
forest (many mixed with Indian),
born to know nothing but warfare
and gardening on the run. With
the children, no opportunity
to teach lessons was ever lost;
nothing deflected them from
witnessing:

Copena, charged with and convicted
of marronage . . . is sentenced to
having his arms, legs, thighs, and
back broken on a scaffold to be erected
in the Place du Port. He shall then
be placed on a wheel, face toward
the sky, to finish his days, and
his corpse shall be exposed. Claire,
convicted of the crime of marronage
and of complicity with maroon Negroes,
shall be hanged till dead at the gallows
in the Place du Port. Her two young
children, Paul and Pascal, belonging
to M. Coutard, and other children
– Francois and Batilde, Martin and
Baptiste – all accused of marronage,
are condemned to witness the torture
of Copena and Claire.

2

Some have said that, compared
to many, when my time came, I
got off lightly. The first time
they recaptured me they cut off
my ears and branded me with a
fleur de lys on my right shoulder.

I ran away again. The second time,
they branded me on the left side
and hamstrung me. I crawled back
to the forest. The third time,
they put me to death. Released
from all my fears now I feel free
to enter their dreams and to say:
You might kill me but you'll never
bury me. Forever I'll walk all
over the pages of your history.
Interleaved with the stories
of your gallant soldiers –
marching up the mountainside
in their coats of red, running
back (what's left of them) with
their powder wet, their pride
in tatters, their fifes and drums
muted, their comrades brutally
slain by the revolting savages
(who cowardly used guerrilla
tactics, sorcery, stones for shot,
and wooden replicas for rifles)
– you will be forced at least
to record the presence of their
(largely absent) adversaries:
from Jamaica, Nanny of the
Windward Maroons, Cudjoe and
Accompong who forced the English
to sign treaties; in Mexico,
Yanga and the town of San Lorenzo
de los Negroes; all the *palenques*
of Cuba; in Hispaniola, le Maniel;
the Bush Negroes of Suriname;
the many *quilombos* of Brazil,
including the Black Republic
of Palmares. And so on . . .

3

Although for hundreds of years
we were trying to stay hidden,
wanting nothing more than to be
left alone, to live in peace,
to garden, I've found
no matter what you were
recording of plantations and
settlements, we could not be
omitted. We are always there
like some dark stain in your
diaries and notebooks, your
letters, your court records,
your law books – as if we had
ambushed your pen. Now I have
time to read (and garden), I who
spent so many years in disquiet,
living in fear of discovery,
am amazed to discover, Colonist,
it was *you* who feared *me*. Or
rather, my audacity. Till now,
I never knew the extent to which
I unsettled you, imposer of order,
tamer of lands and savages,
suppressor of feeling, possessor
of bodies. You had no option
but to track me down and
re-enslave me, for you saw me
out there as your own unguarded
self, running free.

ADVICE AND DEVICES

Gardening in the Tropics can be
quite a struggle if you don't
know what you're doing. When I go
to the agricultural fair, every
one there comes crowding round
to see my prizes. Even the ones who
take advice from the government man
and use a whole heap of sprays
and fertilize out all the taste
from the pumpkin and yam.

When they ask my secret I just
smile and say: Live Right and
Do Good. That's true, for the
world out there is full of hellish
creatures threatening to undermine
you, like cutworms and ants, but
the worst ones are the bad-minded
two-footed wearing pants, who will
do things to harm your garden or
steal your crop – unless you know

how to make them stop. Listen
to me (and don't tell anybody):
Once you find the right spot
for your garden, before you fell
a tree or pull a weed, be sure
to ask pardon to dig, with a
sprinkling of rum for Mother Earth's
sake (you should also take a swig
and rub some over your head
in case there's a snake).

Then, as soon as you lay out your
field, plant at the four corners
Overlook Bean to be your eyes when
you cannot be seen. Should the
evil-doers still trespass (for even
Overlook Bean has to rest) be sure
to burn wangla (but not to excess).
With the ashes, mix a trace of the
dirt from their footstep with powdered
hummingbird wings (for they never

stop beating) and Oil of Compellance
with six fresh leaves of what
some call bizzie-lizzie and we call
impatiens. Wrap up in cowitch,
tie with chaini wis, and bury
at the four corners under the fence
at the exact commencement of the
new moon. The next time someone
(though we all know who) should
take pass and come into

the property to commit offence,
his foot-bottom, his whole body
will start to itch and tremble
and that culprit will have no
recompense, but be forced to
wander the earth, scratching.
After that, your patch will
thrive, for the Lord likes *you*
to deal with the covetous
so *He* can smile on the righteous.

There are other recipes and devices
to use for protection but my main
advice is: never explain,

especially to those who rely on
the plan of the government man
with the book. They are the
chief ones in need of your wisdom,
for their fields (with
all that fertilizer and spray)
will never stay healthy.

All I will say (when people
ask how my garden can bear
so, year after year without
wearing thin): you must know
what you're doing. For instance,
certain crops will only grow
if planted the first night of the
full moon, others should be
planted when the moon is waning.
There's a right way of doing

everything. Take pumpkin. The
morning you plant it, plan
nothing else for the day, for
once you put the seeds in the
ground and water, you must stay
at your yard, lie down and rest
– unless you want your pumpkin
to grow worthless and run around
with no time to settle down and
bear. And when the vine is nicely

blossoming, ask a pregnant lady
to walk all over it to make the
fruits set and grow full, like
how she's showing. I don't have
to tell you plants won't thrive
if you're quarrelsome. Sometimes

I go to my fields and sing. The
birds join in and we have a real
harmony going. I keep the crops
happy, treat them right, so

they'll put out their best
for me to take to the agricultural
fair and madden everyone there.
I don't worry about bad-eye and
jealousy for I have nutmeg in
my mouth; in my pocket, rosemary.
When they ask me for my tips,
I take a deep breath and come
right out and say: Just Live Right
and Do Good, my way.

MYSTERY
African Gods in the New World

MARASSA: DIVINE TWINS

Our coming itself
was a miracle
One spirit split in two
equals one

We grow
We are fed
We sleep
We wake up
We play:

I am day you are night
You are left I am right
I am up you are down
You are young I am old
I am man you are woman
You are death I am life

– Let's play it again
the other way round

– The way it is
in the mirror?

Don't worry, Mother, sleep tight
Our spirit guards your hearth
We do nothing by halves
We are your ancestors
We are your children

OBATALA: FATHER OF WISDOM

Unblemished
Father of Wisdom
Lord of High Mountains:
Take my aspirations
beyond heights
of great men
reached
and kept

OSANYIN: GOD OF HERBALISM

One-legged man
shoots up a tree
root without end
his bird
of a voice
pitched perfectly
to forward our prayers
rain heavenly leaves down

O forest
O doctor
I halloa thee
my voice as tiny
as beat of bird's wing

You know what I need

    one leaf for sorcery
    one leaf for prophecy
    one leaf for healing
    one leaf for the pot

O wilderness
O harmony

Who says
one hand cannot balance
one leg cannot dance
one eye cannot witness
one ear cannot divine

the permutations of the leaves?

OSOSI: GOD OF HUNTING

The Master of Animals
waits for game

Meantime
he schools himself to discern the logic of signs
    in animal footprints and excreta
tracks constellations across the sky to establish
    the pattern of seasonal migrations
searches for extraordinary vision in plants
    expresses their juices in arrow and fish poisons
unravels the tongues of birds hoping to learn the
    secret names by which to summon them
transports his thoughts great distances into traps,
    asylums, cages, to learn ways of refining the hunt
duels with lightning to improve his speed; walks
    in step with the tortoise to learn patience

Sometimes
while waiting
he grants us the boon of attaching our prayers to his
arrows
and he practises shooting
at stars

OGUN: GOD OF IRON

1

Hand a' bowl, knife a' throat

our sacrifice dispatched
OGUN EATS FIRST

2

Iron in the blood feeds
your red-hot energy; fires
your metallurgy in the
cauldron or smelter,
transmits your power
to the forge, transmutes
carbon into diamonds,
expresses oil from rocky
strata, bends the centre
of gravity to your sword.

For the kill, you arm
battalions, beat
ploughshare into gun,
unleash atomic energy,
distil power from the sun
to shape our potential
for death or – if you
choose – life, for power
is your calling and
manifest its ways:

You forge our
connections, you fashion
our handshakes, our
friendships you seal,
bind our oaths sworn
in blood; for the life
of the spirit is fuelled
by fire engendered where
our heartbeats
spark into life.

Yet, heavenly transformer
of our weak impulses,
you allow our fevers,
the fire in our loins,
our burning desires
to consume us
while, knife in hand,
iron-hearted warrior,
you coolly
stalk alone.

SHANGO: GOD OF THUNDER

He come here all the time
sharp-dresser
womanizer
sweet-mouth
smooth-talker
– but don't pull his tongue
is trouble
you asking
his tongue quick
like lightning
zigzagging
hear him nuh:
I SPEAK ONLY ONCE!

He well arrogant
is true but don't question
take cover
when his face turn dark
like is thunder
rolling
like is stone
falling
from on high
from the sky
is like rain

Just as suddenly
is sunshine breaking
is like water
in his sweet-mouth
again

Is so everything
swift with him
he don't stand
no nonsense (though
he likes to be
one of the boys)
he'll roll in here
on his steed
(plenty horsepower
there) ride in
like a warrior
of old (you expect
him to be waving
some primitive tool
like a hatchet)
When he comes in
no matter what tune playing
they rev up the drums
as if he own them
to play that zigzag
syncopated beat
that he like

Everybody rushing
to salute him
do his bidding
for there's no telling
the state of his mind:
I SPEAK ONLY ONCE!

The girls like him
(though they say
he have three wife already)
he sweet-mouth them yes
have his way
give plenty children

If they want him to stay
they must do as he say
he prefers
hanging around
with the boys
anyway
woman must know her place
plus he swear
is only son
he can father

I tell you something:
If you want
to get anywhere
with him
act
like you tough
that is what he respect
work yu brains
not sweat but cunning
win the fight
learn sweet-talking
be smooth

Just remember
he alone can strike
with his tongue
zigzagging
like lightning

Hear him nuh:
IS ONLY ONCE I SPEAK!

ORUNMILLA: GOD OF DIVINATION

Like St. Joseph
the carpenter
taking our measure
sending back order
forecasting
forewarning
Foremost Diviner
how fortunate
for your children
what you have
ordered us forever
to recall: in
four-square
is all.

BABALU: LORD OF THE EARTH

Dogs herald your approach, Old Man,
the hot earth rises to greet you.

(We dare not fan, nor pray for cooler
weather though on our skin something

is breaking out and threading its way,
like beads). Lord, accept our offering,

our vever of grain placed outside
our gates to save you the pain

of that long walk in the sun-hot.
Spare us this time from visible sign

of our excess – the marks of your last
visit we wear forever on our skin

(with pride, we hasten to say, those
not yet put away in your cemetery).

Oh no, please don't misconstrue: for
whatever you send us, we thank you.

We thank you for the beads; we thank you
for the peanuts; we thank you for the

sesame seeds; we thank you for the gourds;
we thank you for the smallpox. And if

you do choose to come in, we pray you
find everything so spotless your broom

will not dislodge a single grain of dust,
for it would grow into such a whirlwind

(of pox, pestilence, plague) you'd sweep
the entire country clean – for which

– we hasten to say – we thank you; we
your children who are weak; we who are not

immune to invitation; we who cannot abstain;
we who have no restraint; we who succumb

so easily to temptation; for we know,
Doctor of the Poor, if you send affliction,

you also hold the power to heal us.

OYA: GODDESS OF THE WIND

You inhale
    Earth holds its breath
You exhale
    Cities tumble
You sigh
    We are born
You whisper
    The Hallelujah Chorus rises
You hiss
    Lightning forks
You sneeze
    Thunder rolls
You belch
    Oceans churn
You break wind
    Forests wither
You puff your cheeks out
    Bellows roar
You chuckle
    Angel-trumpets bloom
You enter the marketplace
    We trade glances
You whistle
    We dance
You sweep
    We fly
You yawn
    Death rattles

Terrible Goddess,
no need to show your face.
As long as we breathe
we know you are there.

OLOKUN: GOD OF THE DEEP OCEAN

1

In the waiting room
beneath the sea
lies mythical Atlantis
or sacred Guinée

Who knows
save Olokun
master of the deep

guardian of
profoundest
mystery.

2

Shall we ask him?

Shall we ask him
where the world tree
is anchored?

Shall we ask him
for the portal
to the sun?

Shall we ask the tally
of the bodies
thrown down to him

on the crossing
of the dread
Middle Passage?

Shall we ask him
for secrets read
in the bones

of the dead, the souls
he has guided
to his keep?

Will he reconnect
the chains of
ancestral linkages?

Send
unfathomable answers
from the deep?

3

Divine Olokun
accept the tribute
of your rivers

the waters of your seas
give back wealth
as you please

guard us from our innermost
thoughts; keep us
from too deep probing

but if we cannot
contain ourselves and
we plunge

descending
like our ancestors
that long passage

to knowing,
from your realm
can we ascend again

in other times
in other bodies
to the plenitude of being?

YEMOJA: MOTHER OF WATERS

Mother of origins, guardian
    of passages;
generator of new life in flood
    waters, orgasm,
birth waters, baptism:

> Summon your children
> haul the rain down

> white water: blue water
> The circle comes round

> Always something
> cooking in your pot
> Always something
> blueing in your vat
> Always something
> growing in your belly
> Always something
> moving on the waters

From Caribbean shore
to far-off Angola, she'll
spread out her blue cloth
let us cross over –

> Summon your children
> haul the rain down

> sweet water: salt water
> the circle comes round

Always something
cooking in your pot
Always something
blueing in your vat
Always something
growing in your belly
Always something
moving on the waters

If faithful to Yemoja
mother of waters, fear not
O mariner, she'll
smooth out your waves –

Summon your children
haul the rain down

fresh water: salt water
the circle comes round

Always something
cooking in your pot
Always something
blueing in your vat
Always something
growing in your belly
Always something
moving on the waters

Life starts in her waters
and ends with her calling
Don't pull me, my Mother,
till I'm ready to go –

Summon your children
haul the rain down

ground water: rain water
the circle comes round

Always something
cooking in your pot
Always something
blueing in your vat
Always something
growing in your belly
Always something
moving on the waters

Renewal is water, in
drought is our death,
we dissolve into dust and
are washed to the sea –

Summon your children
haul the rain down

white water: blue water
the circle comes round

Always something
cooking in your pot
Always something
blueing in your vat
Always something
growing in your belly
Always something
moving on the waters.

GUÉDÉ: LORD OF THE DEAD

By the sign of the crossroads
beat two turns of the drum
turn and beat again
put the pepper in the rum

lay out the cassava bread.
I might come. If I'm not busy.
Don't complain. You think
I'm just a trickster, playing

the cocksman, joking around,
working brain. Remember: is you
waiting on me, not the other
way: today you here, tomorrow

you gone – if I say. Pray
I don't come dressed in top hat
and tails, dark glasses
on mi face, puffing big Havana,

strutting round the place.
If you realize what's good
for you no matter who else
you expecting you'll still

turn and beat the drum
put out the pepper rum, pile up
the cassava bammy, maybe a chicken
or two for company

and pray I don't get more hungry
than that

this very night.

ACKNOWLEDGEMENTS

The epigraph on p. 11 is taken from *The Scent of Guava: Plinio Apuleyo Mendoza in Conversation with Gabriel García Márquez*. London: Verso, 1982.

Jean Rhys's own words in "Meditation on Red" on pp. 46-55 are taken from: Jean Rhys, *Letters, 1931-66*. Selected and edited by Francis Wyndham and Diana Melly, Penguin, 1984; and Jean Rhys, *Smile Please: An Unfinished Autobiography*, London: André Deutsch, 1979.

The quotation in "Gardening on the Run" on p. 108 is from a translation of the official records of the trial quoted in Richard Price, ed., *Maroon Societies: Rebel Slave Communities in the Americas*, Garden City, N.Y.: Anchor, 1973.

The poems "Fern" and "Mountain Pride" first appeared in my collection, *Talking of Trees*, Kingston, Jamaica: Calabash, 1985.

Thanks to Mike O'Connor and the staff of Insomniac Press for giving new life to *Gardening*.

Made in the USA
Middletown, DE
25 October 2017